Parentally Incorrect

Parentally Incorrect

True Tales by Real Moms About the F**ked-Up Things Their Kids Have Done

SHAYNA FERM and TRACEY TEE

Health Communications, Inc.
Deerfield Beach, Florida

www.hcibooks.com

Library of Congress Cataloging-in-Publication Data
is available through the Library of Congress

ISBN-13: 978-07573-2-0484 (Paperback)
ISBN-10: 07573-2048-1 (Paperback)
ISBN-13: 978-07573-2-0569 (ePub)
ISBN-10: 07573-2056-2 (ePub)

Publisher: Health Communications, Inc.
        3201 S.W. 15th Street
        Deerfield Beach, FL 33442–8190

Photo editing by Jack Strader
Cake decorating by Kate Burgess
Author photo by Paul Joyner

THIS BOOK IS DEDICATED TO
OUR MTHRFKRS, CHRISTOPHER AND JONNY,
WHO GOT US INTO THIS MESS.

You Are an Awesome Mom

As you turn the pages of *Parentally Incorrect*, a few things will likely happen: you will become horrified (sorry), or you will think to yourself, *YES! My kid isn't the only one who has done that,* and/or possibly, *That poor mom.* The truth is, kids are hard. Raising them is harder. We collected these stories to help you laugh about it.

We created *The Pump and Dump Show* in 2012 while drowning in new motherhood. It started small, in a local bar, and we really just wanted to give moms an excuse to get out of the house, have an adult beverage or two, and help push a bit of the dark cloud of parental anxiety off our collective, engorged chests. We wanted to be able to laugh together about all the ridiculous and messed up parts of motherhood. We wanted to remember—for just a few Chardonnay-filled minutes—who we were before we had kids. We wanted to not feel so overwhelmed and isolated. We needed it, and as our crowds grew and we took our show to bigger venues in different cities across the country, we quickly learned that a whole lot of other moms needed it, too.

At every single show since its conception (ha), we pass out index cards and ask moms to write down "The Most F**cked-Up Thing My Kid Has Done." We collect all the stories (totally anonymously) and read a bunch of them out loud during the performance. It's one of our favorite parts of the show because, inevitably, there are unbelievable stories that make us laugh so hard we cry. Some moms stand up screaming that it was their story. Some hide in their comedy club nachos. There is a lot of cheering. Five years and hundreds of shows later, we have collected thousands of mind-blowing, hysterical, but very true stories from mothers coast-to-coast, many of which are included in this book.

We'd like to be clear about one thing: we *love* being moms. We love the loud, challenging, sticky, tear-filled, snot-covered, poop-smeared journey, and we wouldn't change it—or our kids—for anything in the world. But you guys—this shit is hard! *The Pump and Dump Show* is a place to commiserate and experience guilt-free recognition of that fact. There's something pretty magical that happens when you finally realize that it's not just you who wants to hide away in a hotel room by yourself for two days, or that it's not just *your* kids who act like assholes.

Our hope is that you can laugh with the moms who dared to share these stories in their own words, in their own handwriting. These moms are your friends, family, and neighbors. They sit next to you at church. They give your kid oranges at soccer practice. You pass them in Target. You cut them off in car line. These moms work, stay at home, work from home, adopt, foster, co-parent, co-sleep, babywear, formula feed, eat placentas, eat drive-thru, hire doulas, have never even tried a cloth diaper, and otherwise make up the entire colorful spectrum of BREEDERs. These moms *are you* and, most importantly, they are your Band of Mothers.

We've sprinkled throughout a few other fun sentiments from *The Pump and Dump Show* to help you lighten your load, including: Sad Cake—bummer moments that make moms want to throw in their burp cloths; a Stump the Breeder quiz to test your parental aptitude; and our infamous Awesome MOMents drinking game to play at home with your mom friends.

Keep this book for when you're crying alone in your closet. Give it to a new mom to scare the shit out of her. Loan it to a friend who just barely survived her first sleepless year of mother-hood. This book is meant to bring you some validation and remind you that we are all in this together—puke hugs and all.

You are an awesome mom. You've got this.

Love,
Shayna and Tracey

P.S. Out of all the cards we read, the most common stories we found were as follows:

"Bye Felicia"
Poop Picassos
Chain-reaction vomiting
Chick-fil-A playground peeing
Fingers in dog butts

Our condolences to all involved.

Glossary of Terms

HOW TO SPEAK PARENTALLY INCORRECT(LY)

PUMP AND DUMP
Conversation filled with brutal honesty about parenting, often while drinking. The metaphorical act of getting it off your chest. Not be confused with the dumping of your precious breast milk drenched in booze.

BREEDER
Any woman raising a child. This child may be born from a vagina, surgically, via surrogate, via IVF, by mistake, via adoption, or alien invasion. If you have a uterus and a want of children, you are a BREEDER and we salute you.

MTHRFKR
Dads. Because they fuck mothers.

SAD CAKE
A situation, happenstance, or object that is a bit of a bummer, underwhelming, and/or disappointing. Most commonly experienced while parenting. (See #SadCake)

AWESOME *MOMENTS*
Moments while parenting when you have done something you are not particularly proud of that you hope nobody saw.

BAND OF MOTHERS
Other women who friggin' love you and love your kid(s). A tribe of BREEDERs who have chosen to lift each other up instead of push each other down.

THIS SHIT IS HARD
Parenting.

My 5 yr old told his
dentist he loves whiskey
& Coke!

I (mom) recently broke her leg &
was asking 5 y/o daughter for
help:
me — "can you throw this
away for me?"
5 y/o: "I'm pretty sure your
arms aren't broken."

My kid put an open container of baby powder in front of an industrial sized fan.   The fan was on.   In our

living room.

My 3 year old boy brushed my hair while I was on the computer. He used the TOILET BRUSH!!!

My son called 911 when I was out in the yard because he thought I wasn't coming back. The police showed up and everything.

My kid (4 yr old boy) drops his pants, turns to his Nana, shakes his wanker, and says, "Hey Nana, ya like it? I got it on sale @ Target!"

My daughter knows the tooth fairy is not real, when I did not leave # under the pillow, the next day she demanded more # than usual to not tell her little sister.

He farted so loudly while breastfeeding that he scared himself and started choking

My daughter ripped a handful of chest hair off my husband + fed it to the dog. He threw up. She threw up. He ate her vomit.

Said "it's mommy!" while looking at a picture of Helen Mirren. I'll take it. ☺

Crawled into a basket then said "Pretend like I'm a dead baby you're carrying around"

While changing at the pool the other day, my 4 year old son asked me where my penis was. I told him that I don't have one because girls have different privates. He looked at me and said, "Well, it's probably just hiding under all that black hair" my kids put bubble wrap on the first 3 steps of my stairs. Screamed "mom" so I went running Down the stairs as I thought I was dying and breaking bones in my body I realized it was bubble wrap as I fell down The rest of the 4 effing steps to greet my children laughing + recording it.

My 3 year old escaped from the backyard naked (through the dog door) and was returned by a random stranger.

Locked her 80 year old piano teacher in the practice room because she wouldn't give her a sticker. (My daughter is 4 :'( )

Today my almost 2 yr old wanted a baby doll so badly that she ended up stealing it without me knowing. She did so by shoving the doll behind her back in the stroller so I did not see until we left & were home.

#SADCAKE

My daughter tantrums to wear my underwear as her bib during dinner.

he's a sleep walker so he woke up to go pee but ended up in his grandmother's room peeing on her. The Next Morning he told her that her wig looked terrible but he liked her shoes.

My son told my mother-in-law that I think she smells like mothballs.

It's true...

Hid our car keys in the freezer and forgot about them. Didn't find them until after the tow to the dealer and $250 for a new key!!

My 1 year old drank a whole bottle of bubbles *At a bday party* ...: within 15 minutes she was farting bubbles ... *At* the party ... on the grass!

My 7 year old son checked out a cookbook at the school library came home and proclaimed "This is so you can learn how to cook." I cook almost every night.

My 8 yr old stole his little
sisters Barbies. 4 of them.
We found 3 under his pillow.
And one we found wet in his
closet- after he got out of the
shower. When we smelled it, it
smelled just like his body wash.
So, my 8 yr old has been showering
with Barbie, on the reg.

My 4 year old pooped his pants
and hid it for 24 hours "said he likes
the way it smells"

Gross!!

my daughter drew on her carpet.
In sharpie. The worst part isnt
even that the masterpiece was 2 feet in
diameter. It was that it was a giant
heart that said :

mom
+
dad

How do you even
get mad at
that

Put dog turd in Cotton
Swab Container.

I Buy so much wine @ cost
co
my 10 year old told the
minister @ church "my mommy
buys comunion in bulk @
costco"! (what a snitch!)

my kids made me
split an M&M in half.

An M&M.

My 4 year old decided to beautify her Lady parts with hotpink NAIL POLISH!!!!

Our middle child ("ignored" child) used to put everything in his mouth. One day, he ate crayons before a visit to the beach, where he then ate sand. He shit colored concrete later that evening.

Awesome MOMents

A GAME FOR MOMS' NIGHT IN

DIRECTIONS: Play with a group of BREEDERs while drinking.
If you've done it, you drink. If you haven't done it, drink anyway.

- I've had a cocktail during bath time

- I've used a baby wipe on my own genitals

- I've borrowed a diaper from a stranger

- I've laughed at my kid while they were crying

- I've blamed a fart on my kid

- I've hit my kid's head on a door jam or ceiling

- I've gotten spit up or drool directly in my mouth

- I've faked illness to get 20 minutes to myself

- I've yelled at one of my kids and thought, *I sound exactly like my mother*

- I've picked a turd out of a diaper so I didn't have to change the whole thing

- I've said I was going to run errands but then went to go do something for myself

- I've stolen money from my kid's piggy bank when I didn't have any cash

- I've cried at the end of a children's book

- I've eaten the potty training candy next to the toilet while sitting on the toilet

- I've placed a dirty diaper somewhere and forgotten it was there

- I've been holding my baby and at the same time was looking for my baby

- I've cried alone in the shower

- I've gotten pregnant by accident

- I've had diarrhea with a baby on my lap

- I've had sex with a sleeping baby in the room

- I've been too drunk to pay a babysitter correctly

- I've used my kid as an excuse to get out of a traffic violation

- I've said my kid was sick to get out of something

- I've tasted someone else's breastmilk

- I've eaten any form of my own or someone else's placenta

- I've given my kid Benadryl to see how they would react before a trip

Round #1

My daughter thought she could fly like Tinkerbell and put on her costume of Tinkerbell and "flew" down our staircase. Needless to say— SHE COULD NOT FLY!! ☺

I told my son that I have eyes in the back of my head and I can see everything he does. When I picked him up from school his kinder teacher told me he cut his hair. Well he finally told me why. He said "my you know how yous told me you have eyes in the back of your head. Well I cut my hair back there, so my eyes in the back of my head could see!"

My 6 year old asked "Ma" is Jesus ~~was~~ a zombie." I said no... he was resurrected. He thought for a bit then said " so Jesus is a zombie. He just does not eat brains."
-Yeah, kind of.

My four year old still asks if the baby is in my belly... Shes two months old and he will literally be holding her while he asks.

My daughter was playing quietly in her room with her friends - too quiet - went to check on her & they were eating coffee grounds from a bag swiped from the kitchen counter. No nap that day!

When I busted my two year old daughter coloring ALL over her ~~bedroom~~ room she had a look of shock on her face. Just as I asked her "Who did this?" Her dad walked in, she immediately handed me the marker, stepped back and said "Mommy, what did you do?!"

When asked what he wanted on his birthday cake, our 4yo replyed: "Rainbows! Rainbow Clouds! Rainbow fire! Rainbow BLOOD!"

2yo ^(said he) pooped in his bed, I checked and saw nothing. Tossed my pillow on the bed to go to sleep in his room. Moved it to my sleeping spot. Laid down and rolled my face into a pile of poop. on my pillow

Demanded I cut his bagel in half, butter it, and put it back together and then freaked out + cried that his bagel was cut in half + had butter on it.

Had a nose-job in July, 3 days post-op my son used his new head-butting skills 'Antie' taught him to kick start the worst nose bleed of my life.

My 10 year old used his selfie stick under my bedroom door while my husband and I were "cuddling". Thank God I saw it in the mirror in time!

wife was yelling to the kids Asking if anyone knew where the IPAD was — Our two year old responded from upstairs saying here it is mom — then we heard the sound of the IPAD smashing on the First Floor. $800 Down the Drain

She always pretends that her mom is dead when she plays pretend- should I take it personally?

4 year old ^boy woke me up in the morning by dumping a gallon of milk all over me in bed ☺ Awesome right?

My 19 mo son took a waffle
out of the trash and ate it ...
after I had just dumped out
the contents from the vaccuumn

My 3 y.o. called me into her room
after I had put her to bed one night.
I noticed her fingers were sticky &
asked if she'd been picking her nose.
"No", she says, "it was just
    my vagina boogers"

my 4yr old has a
toy chainsaw he cut
a turd with

Our 1 year-old son, Elliot,
Smeared a large tub of
Vaseline on our brand new
sofa. Huge _pain_ _in_ _the_ _ass_
to clean-up !! (microfiber suede
-always looks wet)

My three year old snuck a stamp to bed and woke up with his entire face and arms covered in red Dinosaur stamps. It wouldn't wash off either 🙂

My son (2½) ate candy dots in his carseat and instead of throwing the paper away he chewed it up into little balls and shoved them up his nose. It took 20 minutes, a pair of tweezers, and lots of nose-blowing to get the 12 balls of paper out of his nose.

My Kid
Shit in a shed at
daycare & told the
nanny he was "camping!"

On the way to this show my
husband and kids dropped me off.

*Husband- "Don't be afraid to wake
me up and have your
way with me when you
get home."

*4 yr. old son in back of van — "Me too!!"
#TMFUTMKHD

My son (4) told the husky woman bank teller: "You're such a nice man. Have a nice day!

My 6 year old told her teacher that I don't do anything but drink wine and shop all day.

My 6 yo tried to put an uncooked spaghetti noodle into the cats bottom.

Had a birthday party at the firehouse for my son's 4th birthday.

Fire man giving safety tips:

"When the fire alarm goes off or you smell smoke, try to get outside as soon as possible..."

My son (in front of 15 kids and 20 adults)

"I hope my mommy lets daddy out of the attic if there's a fire"

My 8 yr old told a 5 year old a joke ending in "surprise mother fucker" when confronted, she decided to "lay it all out on the table" she admitted to (in 2nd grade) being a part of a "cursing club", and meeting down by the sewers during recess.

My son got his tongue stuck in a toaster and they had to call the ambulance to get it unstuck.

MY TODDLER DAUGHTER, WHO'S DEVELOPED A SUDDEN FEAR OF WATER, TOOK A BATH SCREAMING BLOODY MURDER WITH HER BABY THIGHS WRAPPED AROUND MY HUSBAND'S NECK LIKE ~~BR~~ 007 VILLAINESS XENIA ONATOPP. HE SURVIVED.

My 6 year old licked the window of the Staten Island ferry.

My Son threw his sisters
clothes in the fire place, while
the fire was going, We just got
home from her Birthday party,
they where all her New clothes.
Mother Fucker LOL

my son said to me as I dropped him
at Pre-K!
"Mom can you get me the
Fuck out of this seat?!"
↓
carseat

My three year old pooped outside and used the end of the garden hose to wipe his ass!!

I noticed my 4 year old daughter was in the bathroom an awfully long time. When I checked on her she was dipping toilet paper in the toilet and sucking the water out!

My 4 year old son took
duct tape and wrapped
and wrapped, and wrapped
multiple layers of the duct
tape around his penis.
It took 2 hours to get it
off.

My daughter told me she was
afraid of the stars on the ceiling.
We put up around 500 per room.
(I have 2 kids) Then when I pulled
most of them down, she asked
me to put them back up.

2 out of 3 of my kids threw up $\underline{7}$ times in 1.5 hours on an airplane ride. And I was ALONE!
(I think I blocked most of it out!)

Shaved her eyebrow off

My 3 year old whacked her
18 month old sister over the head
with a frying pan (play kitchen).
When asked what the heck she was
doing she replied, "I'm Rapunzel
and she's Flynn Ryder..." Damn
                                    Disney...

4yo asked me to sing him "a beautiful
song about my penis"

my daughter told me I am
not meeting her expectations

she's 7

My 7 year old daughter cut her
~~BANGS~~ practically to her scalp, for
the 3rd **FUCKIN'** time in 2 years.

Stump the Breeder

A JUDGMENT OF YOUR PARENTAL KNOWLEDGE

Test your parental aptitude with these multiple-choice questions.
If you do not know the correct answers, you must return your children.

At the very moment of sperm-to-egg fertilization:
A) The mother's uterus expands to seven times its size
B) The baby's sex and genetic profile are determined
C) The baby's father is already sleeping
D) An angel gets its wings and a sailor dies

Some dads experience the same pregnancy symptoms as their wives, like increased body weight and morning sickness. This is known as a sympathetic pregnancy or:
A) Complete bullshit
B) Couvade syndrome
C) Stockholm syndrome
D) Fuck you. You have NO IDEA what this feels like

After giving birth, it is recommended to abstain from sex:
A) For at least 72 hours
B) Until your partner breaks down crying
C) For 6 weeks
D) Until the house is clean

The first book about pediatric medicine was published in 1472 and focused mainly on:
A) Childhood diseases
B) Baby boners
C) Chronic whining
D) The Whole 30

Mothers who nurse each other's babies are engaging in a reciprocal act known as:
A) Cross-nursing
B) 69
C) Communippling
D) Cross-dressing

Redness, swelling, itching, and discharge in the eye is called "pink eye" or:
A) Conjunctivitis
B) House arrest
C) The Eye of Sauron
D) Slightly better than lice

Which of the following is most commonly used to make a woman more comfortable during childbirth:
A) A martini
B) A yoga/balance ball
C) Netflix
D) Her father-in-law with his video camera

The sticky substance on a baby's skin after delivery is called:
A) Glue
B) Kombucha
C) Vernix
D) Uterade

In the course of a minute, the average toddler can:
A) Set fire to your bedroom
B) Open every single app on your phone
C) Take 176 steps
D) Dissolve a marriage

A professional breastfeeding specialist is called a:

A) Titty Handler
B) Juggler
C) Boob Maiden
D) Dairy Fairy
E) Breastaholic
F) Nipple Negotiator
G) Mammary Memory Maker
H) Milk Monster
I) Knocker Nurse
J) Hooter Tutor
K) Melanie the Melon Manipulator
L) Teat-cher
M) Feedbag Fixer
N) Half and Half Staff

O) Old Lady Pump and Dump
P) Sweater Meat Maid
Q) Cantaloupe Curator
R) Areola Ayatollah
S) Leche Loosener
T) Bazoonga Batterer
U) Squirt Expert
V) Mayor of Latchtown
W) Protein Pusher
X) Vitamin D Dealer
Y) Dr. Letdown
Z) Colostrum Coach
AA) Godsend
BB) Lactation Consultant

My 7 yr old completely called me out on a little white lie I told to get out of a b-day party.
He said "mom you were at home drinking BEER" 😣

Woke up at 10:30pm 12:00AM 12:45AM 1:30AM 2:30AM 3:30 AM 4:20AM 5:30AM
Then slept 4 hours straight for my husband. ☺

My 4 y.o. jumped out of the pool, pulled down her bottoms and _pooped_ right on the pool deck. Pulled them back up and went back in the pool.

A bungee cord keeps our sliding door closed - today my kid (somehow) got one end on his shirt & the gate - he looked like a ~~dog~~ on a short leash trying to chase a squirrel. Poor kid. (Bad mom for getting it on video). #momfail

Whenever I sing My 2 year old
Points at Me & Says "no"!

Putting her tankini (boobies out!)
bathing suit top on
backwards + walking out
of the house like it's completely
normal (I have a photo)

When my husband stepped out of the shower my 4yr old daughter pointed to his penis and yelled "Daddy has a butt carrot"

My 9 year old daughter Marley AKA: Gnarly Marley and I were in the wine Isle and she said very loud... "mom are you getting Rombauer? or are you broke and getting Josh?" About 10 People started laughing

My 10-month-old threw up in my husband's ear and gave him an ear infection.

Showering with my 19-month-old son.
   He's ~~helps~~ starts filling up a water toy, using the water dripping from my pubic hair.

It happened this morning.

I threw out my back.
and my then 6 yr old
said "Mommy I'm not
trying to be mean or anything
but... I think your body
is getting ready to die" 😳

My 3 yr old started telling
People my Husband and I are
cousins.
WE ARE NOT cousins.
PROMISE!

Day 1 of living in our new place, my son decided to use a CD he found to open up a can of blue paint— he poured it all over the brand new carpet, and as he screamed and ran into the bathroom, he smeared his hand all over the freshly painted walls & doors!!

My son Owen, 4 years old went thru a crazy booger eating phase, in line for communion at church he got to the front, picked a booger, offered it to the priest & said "Here God, I got a big one for you"

My son peed in a tub
of 1000+ piece
legos.

My 7 year old son decided to
steal rosary beads at church
during religion class. When
he got caught at school the
next day, he paid the girl #3
not to tell. (hush #) - straight to
confession for him!!

My 6 year old daughter said "Mama, I know what I'm getting you for your birthday." me- "what?" daughter "ProActive for your face." Seriously!

my 4 y.o. told a nun that when she grows up, she wants to be a "nipple doctor." Yelled for emphasis.

He set up his legos so they made the scene from Lady Gaga's "Telephone" where she and Beyonce poison everyone in the diner, then he said he was Lady Gaga and his kindergarten girlfriend Jane is Beyonce & they were poisoning everyone. He's almost 6yr old.

My 4 yr old son barged in the bathroom just after I got done putting in a tampon. He saw my string hanging out and screams "Mommy, A mouse just crawled up inside you!!"

My 6 year-old daughter told my husband he could not do homework with her because she needed someone smart to help her.

I once came home to my 4 yr old son butt naked peeing all over his toy dinosaurs because "they were thirsty."

AT AGE 2, IN PRE-SCHOOL
EVERYONE DANCING & SINGING
"WHEELS ON THE BUS" EXCEPT
MY SON WHO WAS SINGING
"ALL THE SINGLE LADIES"

My daughter & neighbor girl
found a dead mouse.
They found their ZhuZhu
pet remote control car
and drove the dead mouse
around the sidewalks.

My daughter and I were at the mall and she pulled the tie on my wrap dress. I had Spanx on so I didn't feel the breeze from being exposed. I literally have no idea how long I was walking around in my nude sausage casing before realizing.

We discovered that our 4yr old son was peeing in the corners of his room at night. When we asked him why he said, " The penis does what it wants to"

my daughter brought
me multiple glasses
of water when I was
sick, I drank them
all before asking where
she got them —
        The Toilet - yuck

While I was getting ready, my 2
yr old (unknowingly to me) wiped
her poopy butt w/ my blush brush.
I figured it out when the smell
was overwhelming while using
the brush !!!

When I wiped my daughter's nose, I said "got your boogies!" She replied: "Hey, those are mine and I was gonna eat them!" :-)

Made a vegetable garden on our nice couch, complete w/ soil, seeds and watered it.

Awesome MOMents

A GAME FOR MOMS' NIGHT IN (pour yourself another)

- I've pretended I was sleeping so my partner had to get up and take care of the baby in the middle of the night

- I've fed my child a "snack" from the car floor

- I've heard crying from the shower, got out of the shower to make sure everything was okay, then realized there was no crying and I had just imagined the whole thing

- When reading to my kid, I've skipped pages in a book that I thought was too long

- I've forgotten to put the bottles on my pump and pumped directly into my lap

- When my kid begged to ride in the grocery store "car cart," I straight-up lied and said there weren't any available

- My kid's poop or throw up made me throw up

- I've spent a whole day eating nothing but leftover kid food

- I've sent my kid to school or daycare when they were sick because I was convinced it was just allergies

- I've thrown away a toy that I thought was super annoying

- I've road raged with another mom at car line

- I've eaten the mac and cheese straight from the pot on the stove before serving it to the kids

- I've let my kid look at my poop before I flushed

- I've forgotten to pick up my kid from school or daycare

- I've forgotten my kid was in time-out

- I've replaced a dead animal with an identical one

- I've re-gifted a baby shower gift at another friend's baby shower

- I've turned up the music in the car so I didn't have to answer any more kid questions

- I've breastfed or pumped at the dinner table

- I've accidentally stolen something from a store because my baby was holding it or had eaten it

- I've given an extra long time-out so I could get something done

- I've had a conflict with another mom at a playground

- I've been walked in on by a child during a sexual act

Round #2

My daughter told my son
to "pee on daddy" so he did.
Peed on his back at the
kitchen table ... during dinner.

My 3 year old went outside
instead of taking a bath. I followed
her out and she then turned around
went back in and LOCKED me out.
She went upstairs for 20 minutes
and packed a bag, came down,
unlocked door for me and
said "Here you go mommy!"

My 3-year-old Shat (yes, shat)
in my hardcover copy of
The Velveteen Rabbit
that my Grandmother gave_m
for my 2nd b-day

My son gave himself
a swirly in his own
pee toilet water.

We rang the doorbell at my sisters house. I said "do you see her" my daughter says "yes here comes the hooker".

My 2 year old took his sister's hampster. I told him to drop it & he did ... over the 2nd story banister.

My 22m (now 2yr) fingerpainted on my newly upholstered cream armchairs with my red wine when I stepped out of the room.

"Mom" "Sex" and my middle daughter's name is etched ~~#~~ into the counter of our guest bathroom. My oldest daughter is the only ~~person~~ kid that knows how to spell the name, but she denies doing it.

My child stuck
two cotton balls up
her nose & I didn't
realize it until she
smelled like death (4 Mo later)

She peed at the park on a
play structure & the kids
below thought it was raining.

5 year old wakes up and doesn't see Mommy under the covers in bed so decided to let himself out the front door and walked to neighbors house and rang bell and said "My Mommy is Lost" at 5:30 AM!!!

My 2 year old daughter ate a glow stick.

She's fine,

My 4-year-old son leapt from halfway up the basement steps, landing on the exercise ball, then rebounding to a handstand on the floor and then falling to a seated position with one jazz hand in the air.

My 2 year old son took the used tampon applicators out of the trash can and walked around with "extend-o-fingers"

YOU CHECK ON YOUR BABY AND WAKE YOUR BABY

My 2½ year old twins decided it would be a good idea to take their sisters water bottle out of her lunch box, pee in it and put it back. :(

Yuck

Me: Where is Tana (our dog)?

5YO Son: Oh she's probably wiping her butt on your bed.

Me: What about Nico (other dog)?

5YO Son: He's wiping his penis across your pillow.

My three year old discovered that his penis fits through the ring on the end of the measuring spoon

We realized our daughter was too old to be showering with her dad anymore when she looked directly at his penis with a disgusted face and said "I sure wouldn't want to eat THAT for breakfast!"

While trying on bras my four year old told me they need to make them longer because my boobies go really low.

They didn't always!!!

A squirrel was running across the street. I did not hit it, but the car coming in the opposite direction fucking nailed it. I cringed and my daughter exclaimes "got him!"

Peed in the humidifier.

left freezer open after
getting a popsicle, and
ruined 4 months of frozen
BREASTMILK!

Wouldn't leave the house until I put both shoes on one foot.

While on the toilet told me that she needed a hug to squeeze out her poop.

Our daughter super-glued our infant son's pj's to his legs.

My 3 year old daughter Farted in the middle of a huge family dinner when my father-in-law was giving a toast and then shouted "Abra-cadabra"

We take our 3 year old son to pee everynight before we go to sleep so he doesn't wet the bed. Last week when I was pushing his butt foward so he didnt piss all over the place, he shit in my hand. Half asleep, eyes closed, shit in my hand.

my son yelled "good bye old lady who can't walk"... to a <u>man</u> in a wheelchair.

My four year old son stabbed the neighbors leather car seats with a pocket knife!

He (my oldest 5½ yrs) told me a penis is called that b/c you pee out of it but a vagina should be called ugly b/c it's just ugly.
I thought I hope you don't always think that! Ha

I was nursing my 9month old on an airplane with a blanket over our heads—so it was dark—and he farted. I was hot boxed by a 9 month old.

He pooped in the bathtub, picked it out and left it laying on the soap dish for his dad to Reach for later that night.

My 7 year old snuck bright red lipstick and applied it prior to 1st grade spring pictures.

My son told me "you are going to die when you get old tomorrow..."

My 2year old got himself stuck in a Weight machine + I had to spray him down with PAM to wiggle him out.

My middle child has always been obsessed with his baby brother, Huck. oliver would rush home from preschool to hold him, take care of him, etc The first time I took Huck out of the house for a few hours, I came home to a hysterical Oliver who had decorated the house with tombstones that said RIP HUCK

3 yr old locked husband and husband's friend out of house so the two girls could go in pantry and eat cookies. They MADE SURE THAT _all_ doors were locked including garage. Husbands finally got in once cookies were gone.

— This WAS A DAD'S PlAYdate
— Mom's were NoTthere

Most Fucked up (BOYS) EVER! My Kids peed in my hair spray bottle. Sprayed it all over my hair and realized I smeld like an urinal.

We were at a friends farm out in country. My son went behind their barn, pulled down his pants, squatted into position, and STILL shit his pants. Like shit his pants full, then pulled them back up like no big deal. Smeary shit pants, yay!

He is 2.5 years old and told his nanny yesterday "I really like your boobies" as she was leaning over strapping him in the car seat

While at a wedding in a secluded church w/ NO bathroom, my daughter had a blow out all over my cream sweater! 3 HRS FROM HOME

My Abby darling drew hearts all over my car for my birthday ...with a rock.

Lies We Tell Ourselves Before We Have Kids

Okay, time to fess up. Did you think you knew exactly how things were gonna go down when you became a parent? It's just us here, so admit it: did you *actually roll your eyes* while watching other frazzled parents try to wrangle their kids and then say to yourself, *How hard is it to just take a shower and put on some lipstick?* Do you know what you were doing to yourself? You were lying.

Below is a little list of lies. These are the lies we told ourselves BEFORE we started raising humans, before we had a clue, when we were filled with all the parental optimism and confidence in the world. We even turned it into a song in our show so everyone can sing about these together, because chances are you've told yourself a few of these lies, too. So enjoy the throwbacks to your former, clueless self, and realize how far you've come!

1. I'll have a weekly date night

A promise you make with your partner pre-baby that also costs more money, time, and energy than you have.

2. I'll breastfeed until I'm ready to stop

This may be true for some lucky mamas, and may be touted to be true by every site you Google in your despair, but sometimes breastfeeding doesn't work out exactly like you planned. And they grow up anyway.

3. I'll still have disposable income

No you won't. Because of Pinterest.

4. I'll have time to hit the gym

Sure you will. You'll go to a gym with free childcare, where your baby is always happy, never has a blow out, and never leaves with rotavirus. So, when hell freezes over . . .

5. I'll only feed my children organic food

You will try, God bless you.

6. I won't want an epidural

Even if you successfully birth at home in a tub surrounded by midwives, doulas, and fairies, at some point during the process you will want an epidural.

7. Unisex toys only

No progressive parent wants to perpetuate the "pink for girls, blue for boys" stigma, but it's scientifically proven that the harder you try to keep your daughter away from baby dolls, the more princess dresses she will wear and refuse to take off.

8. I'll just bring the baby in the shower with me

Two things about this: 1) You deserve five minutes to yourself; and 2) Babies are slippery.

9. I'll have a social life

Yes you will—but not with your friends. With a glass of wine.

10. My breasts will stay the same

Hahahahahahahahahahahahahahahahahahahahahahahahahahahahahahahahahaha!!!!!!

I was using the restroom at the movie
theater and was having my period.
I had to bring my sons 8, 4 into
the family restroom. My 8 year old
upon seeing the blood he is not
"fimiliar" with opened the bathroom
+ screamed for someone to call an
ambulance because I was bleeding
to death.

My 3 year old drew a picture
of me like this -
I asked her what that is...
she said " That big hairy thing
you always pee out of "

I had to ask one of my twins to take his penis off of the t.v.

After several minutes of hearing loud "thumps" coming from the bathroom, I went to investigate only to find my 2 year old covered head to toe in mommy's lube. I went to console her because I could not figure out why she was crying and upset. Turns out, the lube had created a "slip and slide" situation, so every time she tried to take a step she would slip and fall creating the "thump." Side note - lube does not come out of dirty clothes laying on the bathroom floor.

At Thanksgiving when my son was 3, right after we said the blessing & he got his food, he loudly said "I'm going to fuck up these mashed potatoes"

My 3-year old was on his 3rd piece of pizza when he said "I need to poop to make more Room". He left the table, shit, and came back for his 4th piece.

my 4 year old will not stay in bed. recently i found her at 11:30pm covered head to toe in vaseline. She had to "put her makeup on"

My daughter asked Santa for "Boobs and a Butler" - last Christmas to my complete horror in front of my mom and in laws. Awesome.

MY 8 YR OLD DAUGHTER
SAID THAT WHEN SHE NEEDS
TO BREAK UP WITH HER
BOYFRIEND THAT SHE'LL JUST
"SEND HIM A FART IN THE MAIL"

My naked ^3 year old Son was sitting on my
hope chest. I told him to get down &
get dressed. He got down, but didn't
get dressed until he smelled where
he was sitting first. GROSS.

Kid #1 in foam pit @ a gymnastic center. Kid #2 jumps into the same foam pit.

Kid #2 splits her chin open (glued shut)

Kid #1 - head is split open requiring staples.

Mom is on crutches. Dad is out of town.

Kid #3 observes...

"Pop-pop plays trains with me". Pop-pop has been dead for a year.

My son Mason
was talking about nuts at dinner.
I asked him "What nuts" b/c
we did not have nuts for dinner
He stood on his chair and
pointed to his crotch + said
"Deez Nuts". He's 5.

Pulled a piece of
bacon out of his
mouth at lunch. We
had bacon for breakfast.

My son offered me a piece of English muffin, but when I opened my mouth, he instead ate the English muffin + shoved dog food into my mouth, which he had stealthily concealed in his other hand.

completely silent restaurant...

he shouts out

"Bitch please!"

He was two

My Son wonders why he
cant lick his weiner like
the dog does. He tries everynight
sitting in the shower.
 He Just turned 4

My son (when he was in)
Kindergarten) told his teacher
he couldn't do the art project
because he was on his
 Period ☺

My daughter saw an older
woman tanning poolside +
loudly exclaimed to me (within
ear shot of the woman)
"mommy she looks just like
our ~~old~~ old leather couch"

"My butt hole feels just
like my belly button"

My 4 year old son Conor told me he knew who was responsible for killing MLK
- his friend JP's mother!

told the Dr he was gross for pulling the underwear down during a physical.

I spent 45 minutes looking for the Remote, only to find my daughter had hidden it in her *poopy* diaper.

While his soccer team was giving high fives to the winning team, my son chose to go knock everyone down because he was mad his team lost.

My daughter's fish was swimming erratically, and randomly floating. In an effort to prepare her, we warned her that it may soon be the fish's time to go. Several days passed, until she solemnly brought me the bowl, and said, "It is time." We buried the fish alive.

At a family gathering my daughter offered my father my large pink vibrater to ease his stiff neck.

Pooped in his diaper and it was 3am + i had no contacts in. Didn't realize it and squeezed his poop nuggets in my hand. Was so tired i threw it on the floor and went back to bed.

My son (5 years old) wears a yarn Jack Sparrow wig and calls himself "Megan the Yoga Instructor". Namaste.

#SADCAKE

GLITTER
IN
THE
LAUNDRY

My daughter was petting my newborn's head and said, "It's so soft, I just want to take it off & lay on it."

She put 15 towels out on the floor and layered them with a tube of sunscreen between each on top of each other.

"Raise your hand if your moms not dead."

My 4 yr. old casually says at lunch today. My husbands mom passed away 5 yrs ago. — too soon? 🙂

After hearing that Elvis Presley died on the toilet, my daughter said "No way... if you could die from sitting on the toilet, my mom would have been dead a long time ago.

My 3 young boys were playing outside + found a patch of sand. they asked me for water + I said no. So instead they pissed on the sand + smeared the mud it made all over each other.

My girls gave each other haircuts. My 4 year old had a buzz cut for bangs.

My daughter was sick and we were next in line at the pharmacy to get her medicine when she needed to puke; so she puked into my jacket pocket. We got her medicine and went home afterwards.

My 16 yr old son explained to a <u>large</u> group of my coworkers: If you're in a hurry just splash a little water on your dick, then you're good!

My son (4yr) smelled my underwear, while I was wearing them :) super akward

My daughter was jumping up and down with excitement at school pick up and announced to everyone, "Mom! You're not wearing exercise clothes!"

Started moaning when I was wiping his butt and said 'can you press harder and get that itch!'

STARTED THROWING A TANTRUM WANTING ME TO MAKE HER A QUESADILLA WITHOUT ANY CHEESE!!

Whenever my daughter[4] gets mad at me, she says things to try and hurt my feelings, like "I'm gonna move to New York City and be a pop star and drive a race car." That sounds like an awesome life!

"You're not a very good mommy. I know you think you are, but you're not."
~ my 6 year old ♡

Awesome MOMents

A GAME FOR MOMS' NIGHT IN (last call)

- I've forgotten diapers and had to leave where we were because there was poop everywhere
- I've left the baby in the car while I used an ATM
- I've forgotten to latch the baby in the car seat before driving the car
- I've put my kid in front of the TV or tablet so I could go have sex
- I've forgotten to turn on the baby monitor
- I've seen or felt pee in my kid's bed and didn't change the sheets
- I've napped when my kid napped
- My kid has taken a drink from my cocktail when I wasn't looking
- I never wrote thank-you notes for my kid's birthday presents
- I've found a toy or clothes in my house and have absolutely no idea where they came from
- I've forgotten to close the baby gate and my kid fell down the stairs
- My kid has given me a black eye
- I've given my kid something to play with that they immediately injured themself or someone else with
- I've forgotten to close the diaper pail overnight and walked into a "wall of shit" smell in the morning
- I've found my kid playing with my vibrator as a toy
- I've let my kid play or chew on my car keys and then couldn't find them
- I've forced my kid to listen to music I wanted to listen to by pretending it's a fun kid song and then danced around like an idiot
- I've burned a meal because of/while dealing with my kid
- I've done everything in my physical power to prevent my kid from sitting/touching/licking a disgusting public toilet seat—including sacrificing my own purse
- I've cursed at my child in a moment of passion or frustration (example: *Don't fuck with me!*)
- I've been caught on the front or back porch drinking or smoking immediately after bedtime when my kid decided to get up and see where I was
- I've peed my pants while pregnant or postpartum
- I've given my kids a treat just to shut them up even though they were being awful
- I've forgotten to feed my kid breakfast
- I've offered wine to a babysitter

Round #3

Cut out a bottle of tequila and a donut for a "things we eat" collage at daycare

My son and husband were taking a bath together. My son had diarrhea, which made my husband trow up, which then made Tucker throw-up! I had to clean up both sets of throw up, the shit, and then shower them both!

I was taking a bath
with my 3 year old
when he promptly told
me to get out because
vaginas can't swim.

My kid made a purse out of
papertowels and had 5 pieces
of bacon stashed in it... in his
bed! WTF?! (found it 3 days after
I last cooked bacon.) :"

My 2.5 year old pooped in the potty but wanted "privacy". After she told me she didn't need to be wiped. When I asked her what she used, she showed me a blanket, hand towel and rainboot. Awesome.

My 2 year old opened 7 lbs of shredded cheese while driving home. There is still cheese in the car weeks later.

My son pooped behind the curtains of our guest room to "leave a present for when Grandma comes"

We promised our daughter that we would take her to Olive Garden (noodles are her favorite!) If she did well at the mall. She did well so we took her. We went to sit down at our table There was an Asian couple sitting next to us. she looked around and said (loudly) "I didn't want to go to a Chinese restaurant!"

Put the Cat in the dryer to see if it made him fluffer -

Put the Cat in the freezer the next day to Cool him off - Said he was not.

As an experiment, my daughter put her pajamas in the valet dry cleaning bag to see if it would come back $10 later, it did.

We have to ~~make~~ lock my daughter in her room @ bedtime to riot come up the stairs in the dark. She removed the safety cover from the outlet and used it to unlock the door and get out of her room. AND SHE'S 2!

My daughter peed on her brother's head when he was buried in the sand at the beach!

My 3 year old fed
My 1 year old three
pieces of popcorn (actually
rocks)

My 3 year old son asked to
have his next birthday party
at a cemetary.

I was taking a shower.
My son kept yelling my name.
He walked in the bathroom
opened up the shower curtain
and yelled "my eyes!!!"
when he saw me – 3 year old

My son walked in on
my husband using the
restroom and told me
"Dad looks like a fat baby"

At ~~Easter~~ Xmas service, the pastor called up the children for a kids portion of the service. The pastor asked my daughter, "What exciting thing happened last night?" He was expecting her to say "Santa came." But, instead, my 4-yr-old told him and the whole church, "My sister pooped in the tub."

When given grape juice at lunch bunch our 6 yr old daughter asked her teacher, "Is this cabernet?" :)

Asked the cashier at Walmart why she had a butt in her shirt ...., it was cleavage

My 3 yr. old son's preschool teacher asked him his full name. He replied "Wesley Alexander Get In Here!"

During a conference call, my 5yr old son interrupted me by putting his cold hands on my arm - which he explained with:
" I had to wash my hands bc I touched my pee-pee. I touched my pee-pee bc it was stuck. It folded over on itself and it was so sticky & sweaty. So I had to pull my pee-pee apart and it just got stuck again! So, I had to wash my hands."
My clients' response: "......"

On mother's day, I asked my son what he got me for a gift. My 7 year old said here's your gift and turned around, pulled his pants down and farted. Then said "Happy Mother's Day!"

I took my son to urgent care because he got a pea stuck up his nose. When the doctor got it out, my son put it right in his mouth. 😆

My 1 yr old threw up all over herself + car seat in Aldi Parking lot and = still went into the store w/ her wrapped in Blanket.

My 3 year old son reached into my 18 month old daughter diaper and pulled out her poop! He said, "Poop goes into the toilet!"

My 3 yr old Lydia came at me waving a tampon.

Me: Lydia, why do you have a tampon?

Lydia: It's a lightsaber. I make you bleed.

If you only knew Lydia...

My sweet toddler fed
her boogers to the
kitty cat princess poster
next to her bed.

I WAS IN THE DOCTORS OFFICE AND
GAVE my 2 year OLD my i.phone TO
OCCUPY Himself, HE HAD my BIRTHING
VIDEO ON LOUD AND WAS LAUGHING.
THERE WAS NOTHING I COULD DO
BECAUSE I WAS IN THE MIDDLE
OF A Pap Smear!

My 6 yr old daughter asked me, "Mum, can you eat people when they die... like chicken?"

When asked in Sunday school what does your daddy do for a living, my son said "my dad drinks beers and pees on trees."

As I was tucking him into bed my son, Leo, hugged me + sa'd, "Mommy. I changed my mind. I don't want to marry you. I want someone younger who will last longer."

My 4-year old son is obsessed with rubber gloves. He steals them from daycare + hoards them. He sleeps with them, He rubs them on his face, plays with them, etc. If someone new is coming over, he tells me he is hiding his gloves so no one sees them.

My oldest, when asked by my 3 year old who the kid was. who came in the photo frame (the stock photo) replied... "That's Timmy. He was our brother before you. Mom and dad didn't have room for all of us, so they had to give him away..." To this day, they still have him convinced that there is a 5th brother who was sent to a farm in WYOMING, He's traumatized

Told me that Ellen & Kellen's mom thinks I'm a crappy mom.

She's 4 and Ellen & Kellen are her imaginary friends. :|

Acknowledgements

Thank you to our incredibly supportive husbands and our very patient and amazing children, who are the real inspiration for all of this. You've made our lives beautiful and hilarious. We wouldn't even have a joke to tell without you.

Thank you to our own moms and dads for parenting us—even as adults—but especially when we sucked as kids. We know how hard that is. And thank you for loving our own offspring just the same. Or more.

Thank you to badass women Carley Roney, Lannie Garrett, Wende Curtis, and Colleen Quinn, all of whom supported us from the beginning and helped open so many doors that have helped the show to grow.

Thank you to Mike Raftery for your patience—you taught us how to put on our Big-Girl Pants.

Thank you to our lawyer, Judith Karfiol, who is far more than just our lawyer. We are lucky to have found you.

To the wonderful women of Denver's the mama'hood. You sparked our fire back in the early days and we cannot imagine *The Pump and Dump Show* without you. You are family.

To Nato Green—one of our favorite MTHFKRS—and to Teri Barton Gregg, thank you both for your advice, support, introductions, and talent.

Many thanks to team ezpz—especially Lindsey Laurain and Paul Joyner. You have supported us with time, talent, ideas, love, resources, sushi, and wine from day one.

To Jen McLellan—truly a BREEDER on a mission—thank you for including us on your journey.

To Christine Belleris and the HCI team, thank you for wholeheartedly taking our quirky project under your wing and getting us.

To Nicole Greene and Debbie Keller at Personal Publicity, thank you for working so hard and being our constant cheerleaders.

A HUGE thank you to Kate Burgess, the gorgeous, brilliant glue that holds *The Pump and Dump Show* together: Manager, Booker, Admin, Sponsorship Director, Middle Seat Sitter, Cold Caller, Internet Doctor, Hotel Room Cot Sleeper, General Organizer, Keeper of the Boxes, Shipper of Boxes, Excel Spreadsheet Maker, Clothes Loaner, Merch Seller, Encourager, Recipe Sender, Checklist Maker, Cake Decorator, and one of the dearest most loyal friends we could ever hope for. There isn't a hat you haven't worn or wouldn't wear. You are a talented and incredibly capable woman. We love you.

And lastly, our show and our book would not exist without all of the awesome moms—including all our fabulous and supportive friends—who have attended our shows over the years. Not only did you give us these stories, you have inspired us daily, made us laugh and cry, and continually give us a reason to get up every morning and do what we do—which is the greatest job ever. We love each and every one of you so, so, much. You are strong, brave, and wonderful women. We are forever grateful. THANK YOU.

About the Authors

Shayna and Tracey have been producing and performing *The Pump and Dump Show* since 2012. Friends since the eighth grade, they each enjoyed separate careers in the arts on both coasts for over a decade and reunited when they decided to settle down with their families in Denver, Colorado. The show has been touring nationally since 2014, bringing validation and commiseration to beleaguered moms everywhere. Shayna and Tracey have been featured in *Parents Magazine, Scary Mommy, Daily Mail, Huffpost Parents, Popsugar Moms, TheBump.com, Baby Rabies* and *The Jenny McCarthy Show.*

Shayna Ferm trained as an actor at The Theatre School at DePaul University in Chicago before building her comedy career in New York City playing guitar in alternative stand-up rooms while producing, writing, and performing in the sketch scene for over ten years. Her music developed into a full band comedy act known as "Shayna Ferm and the Upper Deckers," playing all over the city at hot spots like Mercury Lounge, Moonwork, and Piano's. Shayna was nominated three years in a row for an ECNY award for emerging comics in NY. She moved to Denver in 2012 and now has a house, two kids, and a dog—weird.

Tracey Tee spent her early adulthood acting in Denver and Los Angeles, while studying improv comedy and freelance writing. Eventually, her family's entrepreneurial roots got the better of her, and she parlayed her relationships within LA's growing art and design community into what would eventually become three large-scale gifting ecommerce websites. During that time, Tracey continued to write funny stuff for *LA.com, Ideal Bite, ThisNext,* and *5280* magazine in addition to copywriting for companies. A Denver native, Tracey lives in a quaint South Denver neighborhood with her daughter, husband, and two dogs. She does not yet own a Subaru.

www.ThePumpAndDumpShow.com

Facebook (@ThePumpAndDump)

Instagram (@ThePumpAndDumpShow and @ParentallyIncorrect)